The Don't Laugh Challenge™
Joke Book

Valentine's
➤➤ EDITION ◄◄

Think YOU can win our JOKE CONTEST?!?!

The Don't Laugh Challenge is having a **CONTEST** to see who is the **MOST HILARIOUS** boy or girl in the USA.

Please have your parents email us your best **original** joke and you could win a $50 gift card to Amazon.

Here are the rules:

1. It must be funny. Please do not give us jokes that aren't funny. We get enough of those from our joke writers

2. It must be original. We have computers and we know how to use them.

3. No help from the parents. Plus, they aren't even that funny anyway!!

Email your best joke to:
Bacchuspublish@gmail.com

Winners will be announced via email.

Bacchus Publishing House

The Don't Laugh™ Challenge Instructions:

- Sit down facing your opponent at eye level.

- Take turns reading jokes to each other.

- First person to make the opponent laugh, wins a point!

- First person to 3 points wins & is crowned The Don't Laugh MASTER.

HA
HA

Valentine's Jokes

HA
HA

HA
HA

Why did the seamstress sew a patch on the arm of her dress?

She wanted to wear her heart on her sleeve.

What flower does Cupid smell like?

Babies' breath.

Why did the girl wear two eye patches on her date?

She heard that love is blind.

Why did the girl refuse to look to the left on Valentine's Day?

She was looking for Mr. Right!

How do birds send Valentine's Day cards?

They tweet them.

What dance do teeth like to do at the Valentine's Day party?

The floss.

How did SpongeBob enjoy his day with Sandy?

He soaked it all in.

How does an octopus sign its Valentine's Day cards?

With ink.

How do you make a blueberry?

You tell a strawberry you won't go to the dance with it.

Why did the girl put her friend's Valentine's Day gift in a jack-in-the-box?

She wanted it to be a big surprise.

Why did the boy give his date an odd number of roses?

To show that his love for her couldn't be divided.

How much does a mole like her sweetheart?

A "hole" lot.

Why didn't the skeleton have any love to give on Valentine's day?

He doesn't have a Heart!

What did the Cat say to her date?

We're PURRfect for each other!

Which triangle has the best chances of getting a Valentine's date?

Acute one!

What did the Owl ask his crush?

Hoo-Hoo's your Valentine!?

What has white wings and wears a diaper?

Cupid!

What did the bear say to his girlfriend that he misses?

I can't bear being without you!

What did the Beaver say to her crush on Valentine's Day?

"Wood you be mine?"

What do you get when a Fish hugs an Electric Eel?

A Fish Fry!

Why was the Octopus a big hit at the Valentine's Day dance?

Because he had eight legs!

The Broom always had people falling in love with him. He really knew how to sweep them off their feet!

I could tell the cat wanted me to be her Valentine, she wouldn't stop checking Meow't!

How did the musician ask his crush to be his Valentine?

With a love note.

What does the Carrot think of not finding a Partner?

He doesn't CARROT all!

What did the one chocolate bar say to his wife before bed?

"Dream Sweet!"

Knock Knock!
Who's there?
Frank!
Frank Who?
Frank you for being my Valentine!

Which Animal has the key to your heart?

A MonKEY!

Where did the two fish fall in love at the playground?

On the Sea Saw!

What gift do you give to your date when they don't show up on time?

ChocoLATE!

What do you get a snake for Valentine's Day?

A box of Hershey HISSES!

What did the one squirrel say to the other?

My love for you is NUTS!

What do you call two penguins on a dinner date?

Love Birds!

Why is Valentine's Day a dogs least favorite holiday?

Because they can't eat Chocolate!

Where did the Warlock take his date to dance on Valentine's Day?

The Witches Ball!

The Bat asked his Valentine where she's HANGING at later!

Why is the T-Rex always upset on Valentine's Day?

Because his arms are too short to give hugs!

Knock Knock!
Who's There?
Mike.
Mike who?
Mike you be my Valentine?

Which fruit is inseparable on Valentine's Day?

A Pear!

Did you hear about the two fruits that started dating?

They ended up getting married in a chAPPLE!

Why are bad tennis players lucky on Valentine's Day?

Even when they lose, they still have love.

Who is the most romantic Avenger?

The Hulk, because he's always crushing on people.

Why is the Flash a good matchmaker?

Because love is blind.

How does a Wookie say I love you?

Huurhaaahnruh!

Why do magnets get a lot of Valentine's Day cards?

They're so attractive!

What did the anteater give her sweetheart for Valentine's Day?

Chocolate-covered ants.

How does a spider sign its Valentine's Day cards?

Bugs and kisses.

Why do calendars have such busy love lives?

They have 365 dates a year.

Why do bodybuilders have strong relationships?

They can work out their problems.

What kind of flowers does Rainbow Dash give her friends on Valentine's Day?

Sonic rain blooms!

Where do cows take their Valentines?

To the moo-vies.

What lesson can mismatched socks teach us on Valentine's Day?

You can be different than someone else and still make a good pair.

What did the second number say to the first number on Valentine's Day?

"You're my number one!"

What did the first number say to the second number in return?

"I love you, two."

Where do soccer players go dancing on Valentine's Day?

The "foot" ball.

Why was the sock lonely on Valentine's Day?

The dryer ate its "sole" mate.

The Fly won't leave me alone, it keeps BUGging me to be his Valentine!

The book never has a hard time finding a date, it's always getting checked out!

Santa Clause couldn't find anyone to take to the Valentine's Day dance. So, he went by His-ELF!

What's the most popular move at the Valentine dance?

The Cupid Shuffle!

What did the Seal need to ask the fish to be his Valentine?

An Icebreaker!

What do you call it when a Tiger is hunting for love?

A Heart Attack!

Why did the man with bad knees have a hard time finding a girlfriend?

He was always stood up!

I'm always sure of myself, you can always count on me, and I'll help you with your problems. What am I?

A calculator!

Why are clumsy people so romantic?

They're always falling in love.

What did Mama Bear say when Papa Bear gave her a beehive for Valentine's Day?

"Oh, HONEY, that's so sweet!"

Why don't popsicles give out Valentine's Day cards?

They think they're too cool for that stuff.

Why do penguins wear shirts to their Valentine's Day parties?

They don't want to get their tuxedos dirty.

Where do computers store their love?
On their heart-drives.

What happens when the flu posts a Valentine's Day card online?
It goes viral.

Why did the couple go to the tennis court for dinner?
They heard it had great servers.

What does a vegetable gardener give you on Valentine's Day?
Cauliflowers.

Why did Einstein receive so many presents for Valentine's Day?

He was so gifted.

Did you hear about the boy who got the girl flowers for Valentine's day?

He rose to the occasion.

Did you hear about the candy man and the girl next door?

He was sweet on her!

Why are there 28 nights in February?

Because there are 28 days!

Why did the boy bring the girl a level for Valentine's Day?

He wanted to go steady.

Why was the skydiving instructor so popular on Valentine's day?

People were always falling for her!

Did you hear about the boy who set off fireworks for his Valentine?

He wanted to make sparks fly.

Did you know that Cupid doesn't use recipes when he cooks?

He's usually just winging it.

Why didn't the romance between the Beagle and the Chihuahua work out?

It was only puppy love.

Did you hear about the shark that fell for a fish?

It was love at first bite.

Why did the girl's Valentine's Day suitor show up with a seeing eye dog?

It was a blind date !

Why did the boy scream and shout on Valentine's Day?

He was madly in love.

How do you weigh a ton of candy?
With a giant scale.

Why did the thief admit to stealing his crush's heart?
He wanted to confess his love.

Where do planets meet their sweethearts?
At UNIVERSE-ity.

Why didn't the two watches go out together on Valentine's Day?
They couldn't agree on the right time.

Why did the boy call the girl on Valentine's Day?

She asked him to give her a ring!

Did you hear about the convict that sent his wife a self-portrait as a Valentine's Day gift?

He was framed!

Why did the boy put the girl's Valentine's Day chocolate in the oven?

He wanted to melt her heart.

What do you call "XOXOXO"?

Love letters!

Why did the couple bring their truck and trailer to the church on Valentine's Day?

They wanted to get hitched.

Did you hear about the giant squid and the submarine?

He had a crush on it!

Did you hear about the girl who tried to bribe Cupid?

She wanted him to pull some strings for her.

Why couldn't the skeleton break up with his girlfriend?

He didn't have the heart to do it.

Did you hear about the astronaut who got a card from his Valentine?

He was over the moon!

Why did the boy bring a balloon and a needle to his girlfriend on Valentine's Day?

He was going to pop the question!

Why didn't the two crabs get together on Valentine's Day?

Their relationship was on the rocks.

Did you hear about the magician that pulled a white bird from his hat on Valentine's Day?

He was feeling lovey-dovey!

Why did the couple bring a rope to the church on Valentine's Day?

They wanted to tie the knot!

Did you hear about the boy that brought an inhaler to meet his Valentine's Day date?

He was worried she might take his breath away!

Did you hear about the boy who gave the girl a stuffed Dalmatian toy for Valentine's Day?

He had a soft SPOT for her.

Why did the heart make a terrible drummer?

Because it would always skip a beat.

What did the one Vegetable say to its crush?

LETTUCE be each other's Valentine!

What's a vegetables favorite part of the Valentine's Day dance?

Dancing to the BEET!

What did the Fruit say to his girlfriend?

I've ORANGED our plans for our date tonight!

The desperate fruit said, "I Will Go Through Grape Lengths for You to Be My Date Tonight!"

Why couldn't the cat make it to the Valentine's Dance?

She wasn't FELINE that great!

Why did the bird show up to dinner alone?

His date kept DUCKing his calls!

Jerry the Gerbil was upset he couldn't bring his date to the Valentine's dance in California. It's because she lives all the way in New Hamster!

What did the zombie do when her crush asked her to the Valentine's Day party?

She fell to pieces.

Why does Cupid use arrows to make people fall in love?

Because they get straight to the point.

What do you call it when a bird gets asked on a date by two different people?

HAWK-ward!

What dance move does the Eel bust out at the Valentine's dance?

The Electric Slide!

Why couldn't the Clown find love?

Because he was funny looking!

Knock Knock. Who's there? Knock Knock. Who's there? Knock Knock! Who's There!? Heart! Heart who? Heart of Hearing!

The horse asks, will you be my Valentine? Yay? Or Neigh?

How is a good girlfriend or boyfriend like a hoarder?

They keep all their promises.

What did the porch say to its sweetheart on Valentine's Day?

I a-DOOR you.

What did one ghost give the other on Valentine's Day?

A boo-quet.

What did Dracula write on his Valentine's Day Card?

Fangs for being my Valentine!

What did the potato say to the sheep on Valentine's Day?

I only have eyes for ewe.

Why did the kettle give a Valentine to the pot?

She had the hots for him.

How do you know a zombie likes you?

They give you their heart... and their leg, and their ear, and their fingers, and their....

Why did the squirrel give her sweetheart a bag of acorns?

To show that she was nuts about him.

Girl to her boyfriend: "Why do you have a picture of me taped to your forehead?"
Boy: "Because you're always on my mind."

What mistake did the lumberjack make on Valentine's Day?

He AXE-identally sent flowers to the wrong person.

Did you hear about the boy who fell in love with a fairy?

It was love at first sprite!

Why couldn't the teddy bear finish the Valentine's dinner his wife cooked?

Because he was stuffed!

Why didn't the rabbit go to the Valentine's Day dance?

He was afraid of the foxtrot.

Why did the mummy decline a date on Valentine's Day?

She was already tied up!

What was the Race Car Driver's favorite Valentine's Day flower?

CAR-nations.

What did the candle want on Valentine's Day?

To meet her match.

Why did the boy give the girl a bunch of chocolate zeros?

She asked for sweet nothings.

Did you hear about the girl who made a jigsaw puzzle out of a boy's picture?

She loved him to pieces!

What did the Dolphin say when her crush asked her to be his Valentine?

Dolphinitely!

Why were Cupid's arrows always shaking?

They were a-quiver.

What did the electrician give his wife for Valentine's Day?

A box of SHOCK-lates!

Silly Jokes

Who always gets ripped off from the store?

The price tag.

How did the sun get so many planets?

It gave them a warm welcome.

What happens when a sausage has a bad dream?

Your WURST nightmare!

Why were the sheep waiting at the end of the alphabet?

To catch some Z's.

Why was the cardboard so bad at poker?

It was a folder.

What do you call a broken watch?

A waste of time.

What happened when the apples got married?

They lived apple-y ever after.

Why can't you trust a clock with your secrets?

Because time will tell.

Why did the cell phone go to jail?

It was charged!

What did the sun say to the moon after its Hollywood debut?

I'm a star.

What did the King of Hearts say to the King of Diamonds when they agreed on something?

You've got a deal.

Why was the cookie so broken?

It was full of chocolate chips.

Why didn't the popsicle get good grades?

It was too cool for school.

Why did the wind keep trying to impress people?

It wanted to blow their minds!

What did the shovel say to the dirt?

I'm really digging you.

Why didn't the computer trust the mobile?

It was too PHONE-y.

Did you hear about the guy who was attacked by a sandblaster?

It was a heavy blow.

Why did the father drop his son's stereo?

Because the beat was too heavy.

Did you hear about the illustrator who ran for President?

He really wanted to make his mark!

Why didn't the scientist's theory about light make sense?

Because it wasn't sound.

What animal is best at baseball?

A bat.

What did the boss flame say to his worker?

You're fired!

What did the mother owl say to her funny son?

You're a hoot!

Where does a tornado stop for lunch?

Wendy's.

How did one glass end it's relationship with the other?

They broke up.

Where does a tree keep its spare tire?

In its trunk.

What is a golfer's favorite animal?

A birdie.

What is a potato's favorite day of the week?

FRY-day

What type of tree is part of your hand?

A palm.

What kind of art can you make with your toes?

GraFEETi.

Which animal always copies his friends' exams?

A "cheetah."

How does a hoagie get to work?

The subway.

Why didn't the farmer's son study medicine?

Because he wanted to go into a different field.

Why was the smelter worker careful to follow all of the safety procedures?

Because he didn't want to get fired.

Why did the miner get chosen first by the team captain?

Because the captain wanted the best pick.

Why didn't the man follow the directions to assemble the stairs?

Because he couldn't get past the first step.

What award does the dentist of the year get?

A little plaque.

What did the Fireman do when the Policeman made fun of him?

He went to a burn clinic.

Why did the Dalmatian suddenly run away?

He realized he had been SPOTTED.

Why did the Policeman walk into the bar?

Because he forgot to duck!

Why wouldn't the limousine talk to the coupe?

She wouldn't date anyone so short.

Why is it a bad idea to argue with a pair of pliers?

Because they always try to twist everything.

Why didn't the cube admit that it should become a pyramid?

Because it didn't want to lose face.

Why did the American hit the British shopkeeper?

Because the shopkeeper said: "That will be one pound."

Why did the man get fired from the calendar store?

He took a day off.

Why didn't the forest get the desert's joke?

Because it was too dry.

Why don't steak knives like hanging out with butter knives?

Because they're so dull.

How do lizards always know their own weight?

Because they are covered with scales.

What is a writer's favorite place to sleep?

An alpha-bed.

Why did the cloud love the snowflakes?

They're down to Earth.

Why was the saxophone working out?

To be as fit as the fiddle.

Why is the Hulk growing a garden?

He has a green thumb.

What does coffee say when it senses danger?

"There's trouble a-brewing!"

What did the plate say after helping throw the birthday party?

"It was a piece of cake!"

Why did the soldier have trust issues?

He was always on guard!

Who is the best person to sit on?

A chairman.

Why do belts have stage fright?

They buckle under pressure.

Why do trees not make very good friends?

They leave every Spring.

What do you call a cow in an earthquake?

A MilkSHAAAKE!

What did the doorknob say to the doorstop?

"I can HANDLE it."

Why couldn't the hungry boy get his
peanut butter sandwich out
of the bag?

It was jammed.

What is a trophy before it's
unwrapped?

It's bound for glory.

What do you call a shiny wood table
that completes a race?

A Finish!

Why are rhinoceroses so loud?

They have big horns.

Why didn't the chalkboard take a bath?

It was a clean slate.

Why was the shoe so nice to everyone?

It had a good SOLE.

Why do teachers always put the skeleton in the corner?

They are bad to the bone.

Why couldn't the band go on a cruise?

You shouldn't rock the boat.

Why did the grizzly hibernate all winter?

He couldn't bear the cold.

How many powerlifters does it take to change a lightbulb?

One. It's light.

What does a writer use to make their bed?

Sheets of paper.

What instrument does a pirate play when he wants people to go away?

A-getarrrrrrrgh!

Why are police officers such good dancers?

Because they are always on the beat.

What do golfers and truck drivers have in common?

They are both good at long drives!

When is it dangerous to go to the stock exchange?

When prices drop.

Where is the best place to be?

In first place!

What animal is the best at stopping leaks?

A seal!

When does a clock go to the dentist?

When its tooth-thirty!

Why didn't the van want to sleep inside?

It was a camper.

What happened when the foot splashed in the puddle?

It got the boot.

Why are parades best in the Spring?

They're always on the March.

Two friends were warming up before gym class by touching their toes. One girl said, "Look! I can reach all the way to China!" The other girl replied, "Well, that's a stretch!"

What's the quickest way from A to Z?

You dash in between them.

What did Red say to Purple?

"You've got a bad case of the blues."

Why are rocks so patient?

They have a lot of wait!

Why did all the children put on a performance of Peter Pan in the park?

Their moms told them to go outside and play.

Why are good dogs the fastest dogs?

They stay in the lead.

Why is it so easy to carry a light bulb?

It's very light.

Why did the gymnast go bankrupt?
She lost her balance.

Why does a grocery store never get in trouble?
They're full of goodies!

Why wouldn't the horse stop talking?
He was stalling.

Why couldn't the broom stay awake?
He was sweepy!

What did the lake say to the ocean when they were talking philosophy?

It said: "Wow, that's deep."

Why didn't the investor keep putting money into his laundry business?

Because the whole thing was a wash.

What is the math teacher's favorite dessert?

Pi

What do you call it when two pieces of fruit stop dating?

A banana split.

Which superhero always has a question?

Wondering Woman.

What do you call bread that's as hard as a stone?

Rock n' Roll !

Why did the locomotive go back to school?

He needed training.

Why are trees safer than dogs?

They're all bark and no bite.

Why do noodles not like being poured out of a pot?

It's such a strain.

Why should you ask a tree for directions?

He will give you a good route.

Why should you always listen to pencils?

Because they make sharp points.

Why are baseball players the best dancers?

Because they keep their eyes on the ball.

What did the train engine say when the caboose said something confusing?

"I don't follow."

Why wouldn't the hermit crab give the mollusk a ride on his shell?

Because he didn't want to pull a mussel.

Why did the construction worker take a pen to work?

He had to fill in the concrete forms.

Did you hear what happened to the guy who always looked behind him because was afraid of mailmen?

One day, he accidentally ran into the post!

Why did the musician throw away her table?

Because it was flat.

Why did the news channel keep showing videos of a large spinning object?

Because that was their TOP story.

Why didn't the girl respond when she heard a magical voice coming from the water where she threw her coin?

Because she doesn't speak well.

What did the zombie dad say when his zombie son told him he didn't want to be a zombie anymore?

He said: "You're dead to me," and he gave him a hug.

What did the tree say to the sky after being struck by lightning?

"I'm shocked!"

Why are trees the best cheerleaders?

They'll ROOT for you.

Why does it take so long to paint a picture?

You have to draw it out.

Two astronauts were preparing for a trip to Mars. The first astronaut said, "Can I bring my extra luggage on the trip?" The second astronaut replied, "Sure. We've got plenty of space!"

Why didn't the shopkeeper follow when his customer went down the left aisle?

Because the customer is always right.

Why did the king tell his servants not to smudge his drawing?

Because he wanted to preserve his line.

Why did the criminal bring a maid to the music store?

Because he wanted a clean record!

Why did the manager put bricks under his staff's chair legs?

Because they asked for a raise.